Rooked

Rooked

The Political Exploitation of America

Paul V. Rancatore

LOYAL 9
PUBLISHING

Published by Loyal 9 Publishing, Boston

Cover design: James Hkrach

ISBN (paperback): 978-1-7329809-0-7
ISBN (ebook): 978-1-7329809-1-4

"We are either a United people, or we are not. If the former, let us, in all matters of general concern act as a nation, which have national objects to promote, and a National character to support—If we are not, let us no longer act a farce by pretending to it."
—George Washington (1785)

CONTENTS

QUESTIONS AMERICANS ASKED IN THE WAKE OF THE FINANCIAL COLLAPSE OF 2008

Why did I lose my savings, job, and pension?

What and who made the collapse possible?

Why hasn't anyone gone to jail?

Why is everything more expensive?

Why am I always falling further behind?

Why hasn't the economy improved?

Why are politicians ruining the middle class?

What can I do?

INTRODUCTION

Politicians Don't Create—They Destroy

A *politician*—as defined in the modern, pejorative sense—is simply a predator by another name: He or she identifies the target, manipulates the prey's emotions, then strikes. Politicians are a self-aggrandizing horde that are committed to leading others astray to enhance their own wealth and power. Despite their crafty language to the contrary, based on their actions politicians are *not* public servants; they are *self*-servants. A politician is willing to do anything to serve his or her own purpose, regardless of the harm caused. They repeatedly manipulate the public by omitting facts. History is replete with examples of politicians using their authority to compel others to act against their will because of some "crisis," then blaming those compelled—that is, the *victims*—while proposing radical "solutions" that create even more pain!

The 2008 financial crisis is a perfect example of this destructive cycle. The government imposed a financial mandate on the private sector to ease the government-generated crisis. The private sector buckled under the overbearing weight of the federal government, financial collapse ensued, and the government responded with a federal takeover of the financial industry. Financial paralysis and the collapse of the global economy immediately followed.

This unwarranted mandate caused catastrophic losses, years of unemployment/underemployment, bankruptcies, poverty, suicide, divorce, and/or financial ruin in the lives of the majority of human beings on the planet! Most vulnerable to these impacts were—and are—the elderly, the young, and the poor.

Our nation is at a critical crossroads. Simply put, *we are embroiled in a civil war.* This is a war that has been manufactured by politicians, the media, and elitists, a war artfully executed by manipulating emotions and behavior. Groupthink engineers arm the unwitting public with hate, anger, and vitriol, encouraging attacks on those who do not conform. They are implementing policies of segregation and separation. Exactly according to plan . . .

While for the most part this war has not yet degenerated to wide-scale physical violence (although violence has occurred), it nonetheless requires its own weaponry, albeit of a different nature. This war also has soldiers on both sides, though neither side wears uniforms. It is a war between those who believe and support the Constitution and those who believe the Constitution is an eighteenth-century relic, an impediment to progress in our modern society; between those who believe the individual determines his or her own future, and those who assume the government looks out for everyone and ultimately decides their fate. This war is a constitutional, cultural, racial, and religious conflict, deliberately designed by statists and executed by their surrogates and lackeys (the media, leftist academia, naïve politicos, uncritical thinkers, etc.) to sow division among the people in order to remain in power.

The present civil war extends well beyond Democrats versus Republicans. It is a conflict between true Americans and those who would rewrite America's history to fundamentally transform our constitutional republic. These elites would create an administrative state and laws for all to live by—except *they* would live unaffected, sheltered within their fortresses, protected from the "unwashed masses" as well as the strictures and laws of the statist society they would create! These are the protected classes and those underwriting their plans.

America is embroiled in a conflict between those who strongly believe one's success in life can only come from and through a politician's benevolence, versus those who believe success is produced by using one's God-given talent to create individual opportunity, resulting in prosperity for all. The result of this epic battle between statists and a free, independent, self-reliant, and well-educated people will ultimately determine the future both of our nation and of the world.

We must pause and reflect upon the *responsibilities* that support this great title we all share: *American*. Divisions have always been a part of our history, but as the Civil War demonstrated, our patriotism and our commitment to the ideals upon which the United States was founded eventually prevail. We must return to the art of statesmanship and abandon this present path toward brinkmanship, for the sake of our nation as well as the sake of the world.

All of us have been blessed with our own set of individual talents; it is up to each one of us to recognize those talents and to choose how best to use them. Freedom and liberty, not government control, are the keys to an individual's success. No cogent writings have ever said life would be or is easy. The reality is, life is simply not fair. Those who believe life should be fair will never reach their full potential because they will always feel like a victim. This feeling of victimization is *exactly* what statists encourage because it furthers their plan for centralized government control: hell on earth.

This book will arm you with tools to combat statism by providing an overview of one of the worst political manipulations in modern history and the lessons learned from this mass-scale subterfuge. The book begins by exposing the "crisis" and the political overreach it enabled, both causing irreparable harm and almost destroying middle-class America—politicians of course labeled the root cause of the crisis simply as "the rich," in utter disregard of the facts. The book continues with an exposé of the wisdom derived from the lessons learned from this event, with specific recommendations on improving the health and well-being of a strong, free, robust, and sustainable country that was and can still be America. Lastly, the book concludes with important guidance on how individuals can gain control of their own lives and destinies by resorting to their own, God-given, unique talents.

The intent of this book is to provide an honest review of the historical facts that created the foundation for the global financial crisis, detailing how an otherwise noble effort to enable home ownership was manipulated and exploited, ultimately exploding into one of the worst financial disasters in modern times. Outrageous government recklessness, coupled with an overleveraged financial system, crushed the middle class! Thankfully, the story doesn't end there; this book also provides an exposé of specific solutions to tap into new levels of opportunity and prosperity derived from a source independent of government or others, and these solutions lie within. *You* must be willing to unlock your talents to create opportunity for yourself and others. This is the foundation of *Entrepreneurial Capitalism.*

If we are to be a truly free people, we must unmoor ourselves from the bonds of our political oppressors to regain the freedoms and liberties endowed to us by our Creator and guaranteed to each of us by the Constitution. However, the choice of whether to be a free people springs from the aggregate voice of *individually* made decisions. In the end, it's *your* choice.

CHAPTER ONE

Failed Ideology Creates Pain

The presidencies of George W. Bush and Barack Obama placed the country on an unsustainable, potentially unrecoverable economic and financial path. It is a path so catastrophic that our country is not far behind Venezuela's horrible state, whereas of this writing people are eating zoo animals for food. Sound crazy? Read on.

Our national debt is over $22 *trillion* (includes agency debt). But that's just our operating debt. The "unofficial debt"—including so-called unfunded liabilities, or debt that has already been authorized by law but whose tab hasn't yet been collected from the American taxpayer—is estimated to be as high as $211 trillion. To put these numbers in perspective, the federal government is spending the equivalent of the total market value of *all* goods and services made within the borders of the US. (Total value is known as the gross domestic product, or GDP for short.) The federal government is spending the total value of our GDP *plus* an *additional* 14 percent! This makes our debt to real GDP greater than 114 percent (national debt $21.615 trillion versus US real GDP $18.512 trillion for Q2 2018). When a nation's debt to GDP exceeds 77 percent, it is viewed as not being able to pay its debt; this forces the bond/debt holders to demand a higher interest payment to protect their investment. As interest rates rise—as they are now—it makes it more difficult for an indebted nation to pay its bills. When a nation enters into this arena, financial markets become concerned, and it could create a global stock sell-off. As of this writing, total debt per US taxpayer is estimated at almost $1 million! I would not be surprised if politicians try to manipulate citizens with phrases of "paying your fair share" and extract money from their retirement accounts to pay the national debt. One fact is clear: no nation can long continue down such a path. No matter whether you are an individual, a family, or a government, if you consistently spend more than you earn, at some point you will become bankrupt. When that happens on a national scale, you are Venezuela. *America does not have a revenue problem, we have a spending problem!*

Both presidents' policies and agendas were clearly motivated by ideology rather than history or common sense. Their actions as well as their inactions hurled the world's economies into accelerated volatility and instability. No one can claim to be a conservative when enacting policies that push the country into financial ruin, or that use military members like pawns in a game of chess, or that fail to control the country's borders. Nor can anyone claim to be a true liberal when listening solely to one point of view; excoriating free speech, individual self-reliance, and constitutional rights; and promoting Big-Brother control by an all-powerful adminis-trative state.

Both presidents spent *trillions* of dollars of borrowed money—*obscene* amounts!—on wars and conflicts that contributed to the loss of thousands of lives. Tens of thou-sands were paralyzed or disabled, increasing direct and indi-rect costs on society to take care of our wounded veterans. Compounding the problem were the outrageous bailouts and social-engineering programs that forced more Americans into welfare, food stamps, and poverty lines than at any other time in our nation's history. All this—coupled with trillions owed in entitlement programs (Social Security, Medicare, and Medicaid) and student, automobile, and credit card debt—have placed our country on a path of desperation.

To put the national debt into better perspective, President Obama added more debt to the American citizen in his eight years in office *than all previous presidents combined.* The Federal Reserve (the "Fed") was printing money (quantitative easing) with no end in sight. This was not sound economic policy but a bad game of Monopoly. Continuing this will cause our currency to hold similar value. Sadly, all the bail-out money (the so-called stimulus) failed to solve the prob-lems that provoked the financial crisis in the first place. It *did,* however, mask the underlying problems and provide cover for those who led the effort.

This is not a partisan effort to pin blame on one entity or individual. The problem is much more complex: It is a combination of political partisanship, federal intervention, incompetence, greed, social engineering, crony capitalism, loose monetary policy, lack of federal oversight and deregu-lation, to name a few root-cause issues. The financial disas-ter that continues to plague the world was the result of a program begun with noble intentions but then distorted into a federally mandated social experiment. This distortion was then further manipulated and coupled with creative, esoteric, and exotic financial instruments to provide easy money for individuals who would never qualify for such loans otherwise (the so-called subprime class of debtors, who are high-risk and low-return, and therefore undesirable to lenders—people owning few assets, having little credit, and shouldering untold levels of debt), all blessed under the umbrella of "federal oversight and regulation" . . . of which there was *none*.

This financial disaster has consumed countless lives and fortunes—and it still looms across the globe. Its damage thus far totals in excess of $60 trillion, more than the total value of all goods and services produced annually by the world's economy—the global gross domestic product!

Six events led to this man-made global disaster.

1) Erosion of the Community Reinvestment Act (CRA) and the credit-rating fraud

The financial crisis would have never come to fruition without the new interpretation of the CRA and the fraud committed by the credit-rating agencies. Coupled together, these two acted as the one-two punch that led to a devastating knockout to the world economy. The Clinton administration "interpreted" the CRA to direct banks to stop redlining (denying services based on ethnicity or race) or else face severe penalties. Of course denying services based on race or ethnicity *is* wrong, but politicians leveraged the CRA in ways far beyond this simple nondiscriminatory tenet, instead mandating lenders to provide loans to those with no income, no job, and no assets (so-called NINJA loans)—note that ethnicity and race had nothing to do with this poor lending practice. This directive, coupled with an overly zealous, corrupt, and incompetent Fannie Mae and Freddie Mac—both of which doled out tens of billions of dollars to those clearly unable to repay—created the crippling preconditions that eventually would bring the world to its financial knees. (See chapter 2 for more on these government-sponsored enterprises [GSEs].)

Once these subprime loans were issued, the lenders repackaged (or "securitized," in lender doublespeak) the loans into investment-grade securities, which were sold to unwitting investors in the form of conventional-looking mutual funds, pension plans, sovereign wealth funds, private investments, university/college endowments, and the like. The security holders had been duped into believing they held A-rated securities from Moody's Investor's Service, Standard & Poor's, and Fitch Ratings, when in fact these instruments held very little, if any, value. This great fraud led to the eventual takeover by the federal government of both Fannie Mae and Freddie Mac, along with their five trillion dollars' worth of bad mortgages, leaving the American taxpayer holding the bag on almost half of all mortgages ($11.7 trillion) in the United States.

2) Banking deregulation

Many politicians cite the repeal of the Depression-era Glass-Steagall Act (the Banking Act of 1933) as the ultimate cause of the 2008 financial collapse. Although a direct link between the 2008 collapse and the erosion of Glass-Steagall does not exist, the weakening of Glass-Steagall over the decades (culminating in 1999 with the Gramm-Leach-Bliley Act, which further blurred the lines between commercial and investment

banking) led to the consolidation of the banking industry and
a new, fertile landscape for banks to make riskier investments.
Had investment banking remained separate from commercial
banking, the ability of banks to make foolish, negligent decisions would have been much more limited, and the financial
crisis would have been much less severe. Instead, the bulk of
all banking activity was concentrated in a small group of very
large banks; if one of those banks collapsed or faced a capital
crisis, it would be the start of a global financial contagion—
which is exactly what happened. By giving banks the ability
to superleverage their cash-on-hand-to-loan ratios—from
8:1 to 35:1—and all but erasing the lines between commercial and investment banking, the federal government created
a recipe for disaster. Overly permissive banking rules were
a huge factor in the financial crisis, but the basic failure of
the government to maintain prudent oversight of the banking
industry was just as responsible for the collapse.

3)   Federal Reserve meddling

Since its creation, the Fed has done more harm to the world
than good, and its policies have stripped the savings of millions of Americans. Adding insult to injury, it has never been
held accountable for its destructive actions. Throughout its
history, the Fed has been the primary cause of several major
recessions—it also put the "great" in Great Depression.
Comprising only a few very large banks, the Fed was given
far too much power from the start, and is the primary lender
to our nation's banks. Consolidation under the Dodd-Frank
Act has only made matters worse—more on this in chapter 7.
     Following the attacks of 9/11, under the Bush admin-
istration the Fed lowered interest rates to spur consumer

consumption. However, these easy-credit policies only catalyzed America's culture of borrowing to reach historic highs.
Without these loose-money policies, enabling subprime (i.e.,
high-risk) borrowers to readjust mortgages to low-risk rates,
the financial crisis would have been contained, resulting in a
mild recession in 2003.

Instead, millions joined the wave of the real estate boom,
borrowing much more than they had earned. Once interest
rates eventually bottomed out and turned upward, those millions found themselves struggling to pay off their enormous
debt, or else abandoning their loans, leaving someone else—
you, the taxpayer—holding the bag. Indeed, "walking away"
from a loan seemed the preferred choice, given the fact the
backing for credit was free—to the loan-maker, of course, *not*
the taxpayer—in the first place.

4)   Financial-industry scheming

Historically, the goal of virtually every administration with
respect to the financial industry has been to mandate little to
no federal regulation, allowing stock exchanges, investment
bankers, lenders, banks, and insurance companies to operate in a casino-type environment, in which the house always
wins. Of course, the financial industry's ingenuity and creativity never ceases and, unfortunately, its ability to develop
exotic, esoteric financial instruments has placed us on the
path to financial Armageddon. As these instruments were
poured into a system of such weak government oversight,
no one could gauge the depth of the problem—or the true
costs. Each new day revealed yet another financial disaster,
as a result of loose oversight, overleveraging, and the absence

of any risk-management plan. So rose from these ashes a new catchphrase: the "false economy."

5) Creditors' reactions

Naturally, NINJA-loan holders scrambled to raise funds to prevent their *own* bankruptcies. The ferocity with which they "deleveraged" their holdings sent the entire financial framework into a chaotic, downward spiral. This "deleveraging"—a kind word for rampaging asset sell-off—upended every stock exchange in the world. Naked speculation and short-selling further accelerated the fall, forcing countless businesses into bankruptcy.

6) Questionable accounting practices

The so-called mark-to-market accounting method became the bad-guy red herring because it forced companies owning subprime mortgages to place a truly fair market value on these newly illiquid assets. While it is true this accounting method has its own problems—not least of which is that financial accounting can become virtually impossible in widely swinging markets—the real problem was that there was simply no market for these toxic securities, forcing companies to account for them at pennies on the dollar. Formerly valuable firms were forced either to declare bankruptcy or to sell themselves at fire-sale prices because their balance sheets had become black holes of debt with little equity. Opportunistic rivals were thus able to buy out their competition at unconscionable discounts—in many cases on the taxpayers' dime, using federal bailout money—creating new monopolies, courtesy of the Federal Reserve system.

CHAPTER TWO

A Little History: Fannie Mae and Freddie Mac

A quasi-governmental agency, Fannie Mae (formally known as the Federal National Mortgage Association) was created during the Great Depression to provide liquidity to sclerotic mortgage markets. In 1968, President Johnson privatized Fannie Mae, removing its balance sheet from the federal budget—already under fire for expenditures for the Vietnam War—to present the appearance of a strong US financial position. In 1970, Johnson's administration created the Federal Home Loan Mortgage Corporation, known as Freddie Mac, to promote the ruse of rivalry to Fannie Mae in secondary mortgage markets. Each entity—essentially a new type of government-backed yet private-enterprise "aardvark"—became known as a government-sponsored enterprise (GSE): a private company with the ability to buy and sell loans, all backed by the full faith and credit of the US government! The security of knowing taxpayers were always there to bail them out meant these GSEs did not have to worry about accountability for poor decisions or incompetent management. Both were trust-fund babies, playing with unearned money for which neither was accountable to *anyone.*

Most CEOs and executives of Fannie Mae and Freddie Mac have been retired political figures, given their positions as a result of personal ties to political leaders—that is, by cronyism. Once empowered, these cronies implemented accounting standards that made the Enron scandal look like a best-practices case study at a CPA convention! So polluted were—and *are*—these two GSEs with greed and mismanagement that the federal government sued *both* in 2003/2004, forcing their CEOs to resign and pay over $400 million in fines. Alas, their replacements were no better and both agencies were yet again sued, for accounting "irregularities." Nonetheless, a type of perverse resistance developed and, over time, whenever a congressperson or other elected federal official raised an issue concerning either Fannie Mae or Freddie Mac, he or she was directly targeted during their next reelection campaign. Combined, Freddie Mac and Fannie Mae spent over *half a billion dollars* on political contributions and election campaigns! On April 18, 2006, Freddie Mac was fined $3.8 million as a result of illegal campaign contributions. Much of the illegal fund-raising benefited members of the House Financial Services Committee. Both Fannie Mae and Freddie Mac actively supported candidates who kept the GSE gravy train going—and openly opposed any who did not. Think of that $500 million as a massive slush fund for *taxpayer*-funded political contributions—because that, in fact, is what it was!

The corruption of these two publicly supported crony-GSEs was—and *is*—rampant. Both even set up "Partnership

Offices"—campaign district offices to support insurgent candidates opposing incumbents who dared to raise concerns over either GSE. Some members of Congress even received loans and mortgages at well-below-market rates—and of course, these were the same ranking members who made the very policies that benefited both the GSEs and the banking industry!

Indeed, Congress established an oversight committee for Fannie and Freddie but, unfortunately, it was not truly independent. Each year it had to genuflect before Congress to gain its budget, rendering the commission yet another impotent enforcer. No one wanted to rock the boat, lest he or she wind up without a budget—or worse, without a job.

As for the fate of the political cronies who led these two poorly run GSEs, they all earned unspeakable salaries, ranging from $21 to $80 million, and pocketed hundreds of millions in bonuses from 1998 to 2004. On September 7, 2008, the US government took control (conservatorship) of Fannie Mae and Freddie Mac.

CHAPTER THREE

A Noble Idea Gone Wrong

In 1977, President Carter signed the Community Reinvestment Act (CRA), whose noble stated goal was to foster home ownership for more Americans. The CRA was drafted ostensibly to address the charge that banks had been denying loans to borrowers on account of the borrowers' racial or ethnic backgrounds, a practice known as redlining. In the view of Congress, banks were wrongly perceiving these low-income, inner-city borrowers to be bad credit risks. Using federal bank evaluations as leverage, the CRA forced banks to reach out to these neighborhoods—but borrowers' ability to repay their loans was still a very important factor under the original statute.

Unfortunately, over the years the CRA experienced a metamorphosis, as a result of continual pressure from radical liberal special-interest groups—such as the Association of Community Organizations for Reform Now (ACORN) and the Neighborhood Assistance Corporation of America (NACA)—to evolve from a well-intentioned, benign law focused on leveling the borrower-scrutiny playing field into one focused entirely on outcomes. For example, in 1989 the CRA was amended to require public access to CRA evaluations and performance ratings. This increased visibility motivated banks to be seen as highly compliant with the CRA to avoid public scrutiny and discrimination litigation.

In 1995, President Clinton instructed his cabinet to rewrite the CRA to require banks to make significantly more subprime loans (those with a high probability of default) to inner-city residents previously viewed as unqualified buyers. This occurred by altering the CRA evaluation process to emphasize lending as the primary metric, as opposed to objective documentation of real efforts to assess community needs. Banks responded by precipitously lowering their lending standards to meet the Clinton administration's "dictate" to increase the number of CRA loans made. This rewrite of the CRA was extremely significant, because the subprime loan market at that time was nonexistent. These NINJA loans became the foundation of a failed social experiment and catalyzed the global financial collapse.

If banks failed to comply with the new CRA rules, they faced discrimination investigations by the Justice Department, substantial fines and penalties, and exclusion from mergers, acquisitions, and other business expansion options. Reluctantly, banks granted mortgages to borrowers they *knew* would eventually default. Owing to its efforts as the largest lender in the subprime market, Countrywide Financial was the first large lender to face institutional bankruptcy as a result of those inevitable loan defaults.

Meanwhile—solely to "help the banks," of course—Fannie and Freddie snatched up many of these fraudulent loans, further inflating the portfolios of these GSEs, as well as triggering huge bonuses for their already overpaid executives.

How could Fannie Mae and Freddie Mac write these loans if the loans weren't backed by any assets?

By statute, the asset-to-debt capital requirements for these two monolithic GSEs were much less restrictive than for other institutions; accordingly, each GSE took on enormous debt. The reduction of on-hand capital and liberal use of "Enron-style" accounting allowed Fannie and Freddie to grow their billion-dollar mortgage portfolios to over $5 *trillion*, with only a fraction of that amount in cash backing the loans. By the time of the crash, almost *half* of all mortgages in the United States were held by Fannie or Freddie!

What happened to the loans after they closed?

Promoted by the federal government, these NINJA loans were bundled into giant packages, becoming a host of financial products. The product name might vary, of course—mortgage-backed security (MBS), structured investment vehicle (SIV), collateralized debt obligation (CDO), asset-backed security (ABS), and the like—but the overall product type was identical: a high-risk, low-value bundle of trash.

The packages were then sold worldwide to unwitting investors who backed a broad range of investment instruments— mutual funds, pensions, sovereign-debt and hedge funds, corporate and institutional investments, and so on—yet each fraudulent security type was touted as "safe" because it was "government-sponsored": that is, backed by the full faith and credit of the US government, under the auspices of Fannie and Freddie. As discussed earlier, although Fannie and Freddie were ostensibly private companies, each acted— and *still* acts—as a federal agency, promising investors the implicit backing of the federal government. Making this ruse appeal to even the most discerning investor, the nation's ratings agencies (S&P, Moody's, Fitch) endorsed these worthless bundles with A+ ratings, further luring investors into the belief such loans were fail-safe.

With banks wanting to collect more fees and as more and more loans were being written, Wall Street further expanded its portfolio of worthless instruments, to the point where these new bundles were backed by hardly *any* hard assets. Many were mixtures of subprime loans with credit derivatives, so complex that determining how much risk was actually in each loan was virtually impossible. Yet the people creating these exotic derivatives knew exactly what they were doing. The potential payoffs they would amass meant they would not hesitate to issue them.

Savvy investors knew this house of cards would eventually fall, and were thus poised to capitalize on the impending crash—just as they had profited from the boom. Some debt holders tried to protect themselves from default by crafting a contract with a third party, in an instrument known as a credit default swap (CDS). This became the vehicle of choice for many debt holders and investors to make money and to protect themselves if and when the NINJA loans defaulted. Companies such as American International Group (AIG) developed many of the CDS policies for these loans. Wall Street was very careful to avoid any government oversight or regulation for this new market it had created. Instead of calling the credit default swap an "insurance policy"—which would be subject to regulation by the government—the industry called it a "contract," and thus was able to operate discreetly in the shadows. At the height of the scandal, the worldwide CDS market exceeded $60 trillion—approaching the total global gross domestic product!

CDS contracts were simple: holders paid an insurance premium—albeit not so called—and if the underlying loan or bond defaulted, the issuer of the policy would pay the holder. Many investors made billions of dollars on the sale of CDS contracts, as well as on the default of their underlying debts. Unfortunately, no one imagined AIG—as well as many others—would go bankrupt in the process.

Since AIG was the world's largest *insurance* company, the US government took unprecedented steps to prevent its demise, "loaning" the company over $182 billion—and essentially taking over the company. AIG executives showed their appreciation to the US taxpayer only a few days later, by retiring to a luxurious $500,000 executive retreat in Southern California and helping themselves to million-dollar bonuses! Meanwhile, no one paid attention to whether the borrower would repay—or who would be left holding the bag if the borrower defaulted.

The most important truth to remember about this morass of transactions is this: capital markets are not concerned with morality, only with making money. If demand exists for a product, the market will supply that product regardless of the ultimate consequences. At least part of the global financial crisis of 2008 was the result of the ingenuity of financiers to supply products in demand—irrespective of their impacts on society. As a result, today many remain in the wake of that financial disaster, with the taxpayer footing the bill. Moreover, in the aftermath of widespread government intervention, many companies remain uncertain of the extent to which they are even *responsible* for any of these products, resulting in lowered earnings and excess cash on hand, just in case they wind up on the hook for them as a result of constantly changing laws that continue to attempt to address the crisis.

CHAPTER FOUR

Magnification of the Subprime Implosion

As far back as the late 1990s and continuing up to the crash, legislators, officials, and private citizens not on the payrolls of Fannie Mae and Freddie Mac raised the specter of the possible catastrophic financial meltdowns looming within these two megalithic entities. Unfortunately, however, politics and money blocked the course of sensible reform.

Today, almost everyone who has tried to save for their family is wondering, "What happened to my savings?" "What happened to my retirement?" "Where's my *money*?" Many wondered why—after years of faithfully following the advice of sententious financial advisors and mutual-fund companies to invest in solid companies—were their savings worth only half their original values? Why were they now always falling behind, when CEOs and Wall Street were still making money hand over fist?

Around the world, billions of people ask these same questions. And they want answers. As many homeowners started to default on their loans, creditors to these loans started to lose money. As these creditors rapidly began hemorrhaging cash, they raced to raise money to pay off their own debts, resulting in a mass sell-off of assets. This is called *deleveraging*. Just as a homeowner might sell used furniture online to raise extra cash, corporations sell equity, bonds, and other assets—or they borrow.

The financial crisis was magnified when the countless holders of subprime loans all needed to raise funds at the same time. Each combed their portfolios for a quick resolution, using up cash on hand or selling stock that held actual worth. Unfortunately, because these debt holders all wanted to sell at the same time, it created an avalanche of stock devaluation, driving down prices across the board—including those of high-quality companies totally unrelated to the source of the meltdown. Thus, trillions of dollars were wiped away in an instant, leaving financial experts deeply bewildered: "What just happened?" "Who is impacted and to what degree?" "How much deleveraging is needed?" The questions began to mount . . .

CHAPTER FIVE

The Unwinding

The global financial meltdown was not solely caused by the CRA, but the CRA certainly created the framework for the manipulation that would eventually lead to a truly devastating event: the loss of nearly $11 trillion from families in pensions, savings, and honest businesses. This event occurred because politicians, bankers, and lenders transformed the noble ideal of enabling disadvantaged people to acquire homes into a toxic cesspool of financial products and exploitation of the free-market system. Free markets and capitalism have not failed us and they will not fail us. Rather, crony capitalists, politicians, elites, and greed have failed us!

A perfect picture of this failure was amply captured in the unbridled greed of former NASDAQ chairman Bernie Madoff. Madoff's hedge fund operated with little regulatory oversight, and as a result he was able to swindle over $65 billion from the biggest names in financial services—along with swindling innumerable families and charitable organizations. The message is clear: if the former chairman of one of the world's largest stock exchanges was able to do this, no stock is truly safe.

As a related aside, it's instructive to reflect upon the Constitution's relevance to situations like this, validating yet again why it is such a timeless, precious document. America's Founding Fathers were well aware of the predations and fallibility of man, knowing that, as James Madison noted, men's unchecked greedy natures would continuously drive them to thirst for more, causing irreparable harm to others. Madison's concern, validated countless times, was yet again sustained in light of Madoff's wanton manipulation of the financial industry. To maximize individual freedoms in the context of an ordered society, the US Constitution places constraints on otherwise-unruly ambitions through the diffusion of power and structural mechanisms to cause those ambitions to act as checks upon one another. This is one very good reason— among a host of others—why the Constitution is a timeless document that must be defended. If these restraints and separations of power were not instituted and protected, then intractable ambitions—by their very nature—would seek more and more, jeopardizing our nation.

This is exactly what happened in the 2008 crisis: constitutional restraints on government were bypassed—or simply ignored. The chain of events that followed ultimately exposed the esoteric, intricate system of financial products—products no one now wanted to own, but *everyone* wanted to sell. Bear Stearns was ground zero for the complete unraveling of the financial market that followed.

Bear Stearns did not collapse because it was not making money; it collapsed because it could not recover from its hemorrhage of cash—that is, from the accelerated run on cash that resulted from poor bets in mortgage-backed securities. Investors quickly lost confidence in the firm's ability to make good on its obligations, prompting them to pull out en masse. The mass pullout rapidly gained momentum as the company's stock price tanked and panicked investors increased withdrawal demands. This, in turn, resulted in poorer and poorer debt ratings for the company, forcing it to sell off valuable assets to raise more and more cash to cover its mounting debts and obligations. The company's value precipitated over a cliff, as did its cash reserves. Unable to cover its obligations, Bear Stearns, the once-mighty financial stalwart, was bankrupt.

Smelling blood in the water, Wall Street's sharks quickly disemboweled Bear Stearns's carcass. JPMorgan Chase was first to the prey, buying Bear Stearns's assets in a "dream deal" of its own creation—one in which the public, as usual, was hoodwinked. Working behind the scenes with the Fed, JPMorgan offered $2.50 per share for Bear Stearns on the condition the Fed ate $10 billion in worthless subprime debt—as well as granting the financial giant a $20 billion loan for the deal. Once the Fed had agreed to its offer, JPMorgan then *raised* the offer to $10 per share—further padding the pockets of Bear Stearns's employees and shareholders—all at the expense of the US taxpayer! Reportedly this action infuriated the Fed chairman, but the damage had been done and the deal was nonetheless sealed. JPMorgan had apparently learned very well from the former Obama administration chief of staff, Rahm Emanuel, who'd said of the disaster, "Never let a good crisis go to waste."

Lehman Brothers was next to fall. Its collapse mirrored that of Bear Stearns, with two notable exceptions. First,

certain instruments Lehman was involved in had asym-
metric market impacts; and second, Lehman was left to die
on the vine. Like Bear Stearns's, Lehman's stock cratered
over speculation it did not have enough capital to cover its
obligations; the speculation, of course, proved to be a self-
fulfilling prophesy. Also like Bear Stearns's, Lehman's credit
rating precipitously dropped, and investors pulled out in
droves. But unlike Bear Stearns, Lehman was involved in *a
lot* more than mere bad loans and suspect financial instruments: it was very likely at the heart of the energy and real
estate speculation that caused oil prices to skyrocket to $147
per barrel and pushed home prices through the roof. Some
conjecture that Lehman caused oil prices to soar to cover its
collapsing real estate portfolio—exploiting the oil commodi-
ties market regardless of the impact on society. In light of the
fact oil prices were at record highs while US oil consumption
was hovering at 1980s levels, this theory makes sense: real
demand should have pegged oil near $90-per-barrel levels,
not $150 per barrel. Finally, unlike Bear Stearns, Lehman
had no government knight in shining armor to bail it out:
Lehman was sold in a virtual fire sale.

So why did the government bailout Bear Stearns but not
Lehman? Was it because the Treasury secretary was the former head of Goldman Sachs and used the opportunity to
remove a competitor? Or was it because Lehman chose not
to participate as other investment groups did in bailing out
Long-Term Capital Management? Who knows? The problem
is, once such decisions are put in the hands of government
officials and taken out of the hands of the people in their
free-market choices, unelected "czars" get to choose the winners and losers, creating an all-too-tempting environment for
widespread corruption. Not entirely unrelated to this topic,

it is interesting to observe in passing that no one seemed to notice the huge tax loophole that awaited the secretary when he took the top job at Treasury, enabling him to avoid roughly $200 million in capital-gains taxes.

Next in line to fall was American International Group (AIG). Like the others, AIG simply became trapped in enormous debt and quickly ran out of cash. Also like the others, AIG wasn't an innocent victim: it had recklessly engaged in hollow transactions by writing millions of insurance policies that would yield billions in profits—but *only* if no one defaulted on a loan. The company spent all the premiums it had collected because it never expected any claims. In the end, AIG's complete lack of basic risk analysis not only ruined the lives of many hardworking employees, but also aggravated the global financial disaster.

The rest of the collapse is history, but its lessons should not be overlooked. First is the fact that financial operators—investment bankers, speculators, fund managers, and so on—are very savvy folks, and in a free society no control exists to end greed or to prevent another imaginative scheme for the next exotic financial instrument. The financial industry's job is to make money; when government incentivizes it to do so in ways that ultimately violate the laws of economics, financial crises happen.

Second, free markets will adjust *on their own and immediately* to valuations in securities. When those value changes are clear and foreseeable, the markets adjust smoothly and regularly; when valuations are unanticipated and shocking, markets fluctuate wildly. In the case of the sudden revelation that billions of dollars in supposedly stable securities had vanished overnight, the markets reacted seismically, severely punishing the holders of those now-worthless instruments.

Third, no government regulation, financial "safety" mechanism, or other restriction can prevent basic economic laws from operating. For example, the Community Reinvestment Act could not prevent bad risks—NINJAs—from remaining bad risks simply by forcing banks to reclassify them as loan-worthy, in effect, and backstopping the increased risk courtesy of the US taxpayer. Instead, in its attempt to change economic laws that would have greatly devalued NINJA loans from the start, the government—through its perverse incentives created under the CRA and related implementation rules—directly produced the 2008 disaster.

Finally, markets love clarity—and cannot stand its absence. Why did good companies lose money? Because when the music stopped and everyone had to find a chair, many were caught holding worthless subprime mortgage instruments they had not known were very high-risk investments. Even today, many portfolio managers have no idea whether the financial products they manage have any of these subprime or newly termed elements in them, and thus the markets reduce their valuations to reflect that uncertainty, and those companies reduce their earnings estimates as a conservative hedge. When companies are faced with restating their financial earnings, this creates uncertainty in the market, and the market responds by punishing stock prices until either no doubt remains (i.e., the stock receives a higher valuation) or the lack of clarity is factored into stock as a lower price.

CHAPTER SIX

Federal Bailout Plan

President Bush signed the Emergency Economic Stabilization Act of 2008. This bill established the nearly trillion-dollar orgy of the Troubled Asset Relief Program, or TARP as it's more commonly known (but based on its net effect, TARP was apparently misspelled). Although American citizens' enmity toward bankers, hedge funds (honestly anyone associated with Wall Street), and politicians is well justified, the Stabilization Act was enacted not solely to bail out banks but also because of the fear that the Reserve Primary Fund would go bankrupt. In the simplest terms, the Reserve Primary Fund is the place businesses and individuals place their cash as a safe haven: money market funds. After the Lehman Brothers collapse, investors pulled over $140 billion out of the money market funds in *one day*. That is compared to a normal outflow of $7 billion in *one week*! Investors were panicking to protect their cash, and this resulted in depleting the trillion-dollar-plus source of capital that financed the day-to-day operations of almost every business in America, not to mention one of the largest sources of income for retirees. If the Reserve Primary Fund went bankrupt, the fear was the American economy and possibly the world economy would face catastrophe. Although we will never know for sure if the Treasury secretary was truthful in his reasoning for TARP or if it was a ruse to bail out bankers, what we do know is that government "intervention" usually results in fraud and mismanagement. All of which is shouldered by citizens who are just trying to live and be protected by the rule of law and take care of their families.

The initial recovery plan was for the US Treasury Department to buy the faulty mortgages and other toxic assets from failing financial firms. Adding insult to injury, while Congress approved $700 billion for actual relief of the crisis, it also approved an additional $150 billion for pet projects and yet more bridges to nowhere—Congress being Congress, after all.

Even more insulting is the fact these financial firms knowingly shouldered this unprecedented risk on the backs of the taxpayers for their own gain. They did so because the government not only permitted assumption of such enormous risk, it also signaled to these firms—through the previous intervention of Long-Term Capital Management—that it would cover any wrong bets. And bets they *were.* Meanwhile, corrupt politicians and the CEOs of these "too big to fail" institutions were fully aware of the shell game. The public eventually awakened to the ruse, as well. Thus, it's no surprise the public wanted these two co-conspirator groups behind bars—not bailed out by the taxpayer and then given get-out-of-jail-free cards! Why didn't that happen? The answer is *crony capitalism*: corrupt politicians were—and continue to be—heavily reliant on money funneled to them by these same firms.

The Treasury opted not to buy the inadequate and defaulting mortgages under TARP because it quickly discovered that the problems were much deeper than initial estimates. Instead, the Treasury decided to expand capital injections into nonfinancial firms that were providers of business and consumer credit. This was an especially convenient tactic, considering former US Secretary of the Treasury John Snow was now director of Cerberus Capital Management—the company that owned Chrysler and a 51 percent stake in GMAC. Although Cerberus had aggressively pursued GM for a merger, it didn't want to use its own money to finance the deal, so instead it approached the government for a loan. The proposed deal was a typical example of opportunists using the "bailout plan" as a cash cow for buyouts totally unrelated to TARP's primary purpose (PNC Financial Services Group is another great example). Beneath the surface of such deals lies the truth. In the Cerberus-GM case, both companies faced bankruptcy because of inept management and thus lobbied Congress for a bailout that would save them. It was rumored Cerberus prevented GM from providing loans to individuals with lower (but still reasonable) credit ratings, placing a severe limitation on GM's ability to sell vehicles—and thus forcing the merger. Cerberus was one of the richest private equity firms in the world, yet was unwilling to use a fraction of its huge capital store either to fund a merger with GM or to support its own GMAC. Instead, it approached the federal government, hat in hand, for a handout. Congress refused the request, but the Bush administration nonetheless approved the bailout for GMAC. Once flush with bailout money (courtesy of the US taxpayer), GMAC converted into the bank Ally and received even more handouts—straight from the taxpayers' pockets!

The problem with President Bush's $700 billion TARP and President Obama's $787 billion Economic Stimulus Package, and other programs like them, is that such programs are ripe for crony-capitalism abuses. For instance, every time the Treasury Department needs a new manager to evaluate or oversee a new program, one of the "usual suspects" is always tapped. Indeed, the subjective nature of the government's operation under TARP was shocking. The lack of a system to evaluate options on their merits instead of by the "who you know" method has led many to believe favoritism toward friends and punishments for enemies is status quo for the Beltway—and why not? Isn't it? Why is it that most—if not all—of the agencies, organizations, companies, and individuals involved in managing TARP money were the same ones *creating* the problem? This is why so many Americans believe our capitalistic model is a failure: they haven't *seen* true capitalism, but rather only *crony capitalism*.

True capitalism—using one's God-given talents in a free-market exchange to create opportunities and wealth that benefit both the individual *and* society—is constantly under attack by politicians and special-interest groups. They would replace it with the dangerous perversion that is crony capitalism—the good-old-boy-network type of "capitalism" that benefits only insiders. For example, ever wonder why the federal tax code is over 2,600 pages long? Crony capitalism: "You do this for me, Mr. Beltway Politician, and I'll make sure you get reelected"—never mind the impacts on the greater economy. Now, multiply that interaction by 535 congressional members, countless executive-branch operatives, a myriad of federal administrative agencies, independent regulatory commissions, a host of special interests, and the pages pile up rapidly. This perversion of true capitalism threatens not only the free-market principles that underwrite America's preeminence among the world's powers, but also the future of our nation's children and their basic understanding of how to achieve even higher levels of opportunity and prosperity than preceding generations.

The crony capitalists try to disguise their rogue schemes by invoking the mantra "the new normal," meaning crony capitalism and its impacts are now the norm and make up capitalism. For instance, in 2004 I watched a financial-industry discussion on the "real estate boom," and a questioner asked how long the boom could continue, when the US had hardly any wage growth and hiring was stagnant: Who could afford these skyrocketing prices when so many didn't even have a *job*? Answer: this was "the new normal." New or not, this "normal" outraged most Americans. The same investment banks that had created these exotic derivatives had become commercial banks overnight, allowing them to qualify for bailout pork. But these were the same banks that *started* the financial crisis! Yet in spite of bringing America to its financial knees, these vermin were awarded billions of dollars, ruined the global economy, and left the taxpayer holding the bag.

The level of scorn most working-class Americans have toward bankers, hedge funds, private equity funds, and anything or anyone tied to Wall Street is difficult to truly appreciate. These citizens are fully aware that if *they* had committed these acts, they would still be in jail today, ten years later. This realization has led to mass populist movements around the globe, since the financial crisis vividly demonstrated how all but a select few are victims of unequal justice. If America does not return to true capitalism—free-market exchanges that benefit all, and are based on both self-interest and virtue—then the nation is headed for a cliff. Without a change of course, we are in danger of becoming a third-world society—a society that benefits only a small group of elites at the expense of all others.

CHAPTER SEVEN

Who's to Blame?

The title of this chapter has an easy answer: politicians, banks, lenders, insurers, investors, and credit-rating agencies all created this volatile financial cocktail. Of course, their greed for money and power was completely unbridled—but were their actions also *illegal*? If so, why has not one top executive from the "too big to fail" banks been convicted? While federal prosecutors have indeed sued many banks and corporations for mismanagement, impropriety, and fraud, aside from billions of dollars they have netted for the government in settlement fines, no admissions of guilt, no recovery of ill-gotten salaries and bonuses, and no convictions for any top executives have been recorded.

But why not? Where did all this settlement money *go*? It certainly wasn't returned to those who lost their life savings. Over $36 billion was collected in settlements. Between $150 million and $500 million was diverted from the Treasury;

instead, the Department of Justice (DOJ) required settling banks to make donations to select nonprofits on the approved counseling-agency list of the Department of Housing and Urban Development (HUD). This DOJ pork-sloughing activity was of course not authorized by Congress, and in fact was a violation of Article 1 of the Constitution (that no money shall be drawn from the Treasury but in consequence of appropriations made by law). Nonetheless, the DOJ took it upon themselves to divert *millions (no one knows for sure because there was no accountability)* in taxpayer money to "community activist" groups. Evidence of this taxpayer-financed largesse is seen even today, in amply funded riots whose members violently oppose those not conforming to their ideologies.

But DOJ wasn't the only guilty party. The politicians who forced the banks to write these high-risk subprime loans also have financial blood on their hands. Were it not for the twisted rewriting of the CRA, the catalyst for banks to create these exotic financial instruments would have been nonexistent. So why haven't any politicians been held accountable? It's well known that members of Congress have the luxury of passing laws that will never affect them or their families—but shouldn't Congress be forced to abide by the rules it sets for the rest of America? Or—to borrow from Orwell—are some members of our population "more equal" than others? The ratings agencies are also not without blame, as these provided those stellar assessments of the bundled securities filled with toxic NINJA loans. Their valuations lured many investors to these "safe" investments with A ratings, rather than to truly safer options, for their retirement accounts.

In the end, as the saying goes, "pigs get fat and hogs get slaughtered." Those who saw the impending collapse and escaped made plenty of money for themselves and their shareholders. Many of their colleagues thought they were crazy for getting out, but in the end the pigs survived and the hogs were slaughtered, along with the savings of millions of innocent Americans. In what has become a recurring theme, the hardworking American lost because he didn't have anyone there to bail him out. The resulting outrage is what led to the global populist revolt and the rise of populist politicians who cater to such a revolt.

CHAPTER EIGHT

Don't Worry, It Can't Get Worse!

The Obama administration entered office in 2009 with an opportunity either to learn from history's mistakes or to repeat them. The Bush administration handed off the 2008 financial mess to Obama—not to mention over a trillion dollars of amassed debt from wars in both Afghanistan and Iraq, almost five thousand servicemen and -women who were never coming home again, and a tired, divided nation in recession. While the only direction to go in the wake of these severe setbacks seemed to be up, unbelievably, Obama chose to double down on President Bush's poor choices, turning a bad situation into a total disaster.

Indeed, President Obama resorted to the same scare tactics parroted endlessly during the Progressive movement and the Great Depression: "income inequality" and "fairness" required "fundamental transformation" to our economic and political systems. The exact phrasing varied slightly, of course, but the message was still the same: capitalism is not fair; societal institutions (financial, legal, medical, etc.) all must change to be more fair; and our independent educational systems must all be brought into cohesive, federal alignment to teach our progeny the true path forward. Ultimately, Obama sought to create and empower—through "fundamental transformation" via attacks on Wall Street and more "stimulus" programs (i.e., printing money we didn't have) benefiting crony capitalists, political insiders, and their pet projects—an omnipotent administrative state that today threatens our entire way of life and our constitutional republic. He has largely succeeded.

In the wake of their actions to shore up the collapse by throwing money at the problem, politicians lauded their "victory" over the banks and other institutions involved in the financial crisis, all, of course—at least as the politicians portrayed it—led by "Wall Street's greed." The truth is much less noble: not only did these self-serving political leaders lay the foundation for and nurture the financial crisis, they also profited from it. To shield themselves from public scrutiny, they convinced the public—through a compliant and willfully ignorant media—that the only way forward was to create yet more government. New agencies, rules, and regulations would have to be established, all through the then newly enacted (2010) Dodd-Frank Wall Street Reform and Consumer Protection Act—the great, "corrective" new superweapon against "evil" Wall Street.

But Dodd-Frank—quite predictably, in fact—empowered the very banks the bureaucrats accused of greed! The result was—and continues to be—a new banking oligopoly controlled by the largest banks in America. This oligopoly is comprised of the "too big to fail" (TBTF) institutions, those so large and monolithic their failure would supposedly bring about financial Armageddon. Dodd-Frank has thus enabled the megabank TBTFs to destroy or gobble up thousands of community banks and credit unions, drastically reducing access to capital markets for the nation's major job creators: small businesses and entrepreneurs. This destruction of competition in the financial industry has resulted in thousands of lost jobs and higher unemployment.

Moreover, Dodd-Frank's attack dog, the Consumer Financial Protection Bureau (CFPB), has nearly no oversight by Congress. This "bureau," which is in reality nothing more than Dodd-Frank's policing agency, has inordinate—and unconstitutional—powers over daily American lives, doing grave harm to America's economy. As Oscar Wilde sardonically noted, "The bureaucracy is expanding to meet the needs of the expanding bureaucracy." The goal of any government agency is to grow as quickly as possible to accumulate more of a budget—that is, more taxpayer money. The CFPB is no different: in 2010, it had 58 employees; by 2017, that number had mushroomed to 1,668—a 2,776 percent increase! With cumulative salaries alone now close to $300 million, what has this "bureau" done for Americans and small businesses? It has cost small banks and credit unions over $5 billion to comply with unneeded, draconian regulations, forcing them either to close or to severely restrict loans to their communities. Dodd-Frank and the CFPB have been instrumental in bringing about the economic stagnation and income inequality that permeate our society and have crushed the middle class.

CHAPTER NINE

Recommendations to Prevent Another Crisis

In light of the 2008 financial collapse and the compounding destruction wrought in its wake, what lessons can be learned to prevent another collapse?

First, the "corrective"—but demonstrably destructive—legislative acts should be overhauled or abolished, as appropriate. For instance, Dodd-Frank should be abolished outright—and its caustic pit bull, the CFPB, should be completely dismantled. This process can begin without even passing new legislation, by detoothing the CFPB at the executive-branch level. Yes, this would take courage, but it could be done, and it would immediately spur the nation's economy and begin to heal the devastation wrought under Dodd-Frank. In contrast, the Community Reinvestment Act should merely be tailored to eliminate the requirement that lenders provide loans to those with poor credit. Creditworthiness should be the *sole* standard for issuing loans, not political motives and the road paved with good intentions—we all know where that road leads!

Second, at least to some extent, our financial and financial-governance systems must be reformed. For example, the Federal Reserve has too great an influence in global financial markets and economies. Since its creation in the early twentieth century, the Fed has been at the center of controversy for its continuing role in causing or contributing to economic recessions and depressions—including 2008's crisis. The Federal Reserve's actions have impacted the earning potentials and livelihoods of virtually every American. Although ostensibly under congressional oversight, in reality the Fed is autonomous. Congress should act to demand more accountability from this loose cannon. Additionally, two other loose cannons, Fannie Mae and Freddie Mac, should be privatized immediately. These GSEs have amply demonstrated the harm caused by government when it attempts to dabble in commercial spheres—here and in otherwise-private-equity markets for loans—mixing politics and political ambitions with would-be free markets.

Third, our accounting conventions and instruments must be reevaluated for effectiveness and transparency. As a good initial step, market-to-market accounting should be suspended or eliminated. As noted in chapter 1, this practice has made modern accounting difficult, because valuations become moving targets in fast-changing markets. In contrast, historical-cost accounting—although it ignores current market values—is much easier, while providing a simpler, more stable, and more accurate accounting method. Additionally, semi-illiquid assets—such as the justly vilified credit default swap—should be bundled transparently. For example, a major financial exchange could create a credit-default-swap market, for more speculative, risk-tolerant investors who would know—up front—what they would be getting into. Finally, the so-called uptick rule—the trading restriction allowing the short-selling of a stock only on a rise in the stock's price—should have never been eliminated (a new alternative has been established). The Securities and Exchange Commission failed the country by removing this very important financial requirement in 2007—just before the market collapse of 2008. As a result, rampant "naked" short-selling destroyed many companies (Bear Stearns, Lehman Brothers, Washington Mutual, AIG, and many others). Regardless of changes to the uptick rule, naked short-selling by financial institutions should be prohibited, or else those institutions should be forced to bear any losses accruing from those unable to pay their debts because they have no collateral backing their bet when it eventually goes against them.

Finally, new legislation should be enacted that is informed by, but not a victim of, the abject failures of knee-jerk legislation hastily enacted in the wake of financial crises. Legislation passed upon wise reflection and deliberation—rather than reactively and reflexively—is always a better answer to a problem than flinch responses. Commercial and investment banking should be separated—as they were previously—through appropriate federal regulatory controls to preclude financial contagion, like that of 2008. Both activities could still be owned by a single entity, but strict controls would protect the deposits and assets of commercial-banking customers from mistakes made by the investment-banking activity. In no case should taxpayer money be loaned to a bank to help it recover from financial loss or to prevent it from going bankrupt. If the banking industry wants to participate in free-market capitalism, then it must accept the same risk others do in free-market societies. As in every other industry, some companies will succeed and others will fail. But in all cases, government bailouts should be available to *no* company, regardless of size.

Moreover, US bankruptcy laws must be rewritten. Current laws protect incompetent management by absolving them of their fiduciary obligations, effectively rewarding dishonest behavior. But bankruptcy should be a company's last option, not the go-to choice to shed debt and dishonor commitments. Bankruptcy laws should be written to provide better incentives for companies to maintain their integrity and promises, not to shoulder innocent taxpayers with the debt burdens associated with breaking those promises.

Preventing another financial collapse like that of 2008 is possible, but it will take courage and perseverance. Bad laws—like Dodd-Frank and CRA (as amended)—must be overturned, and new laws must be enacted that protect the free market and punish market malefactors. Accounting standards must reflect realities in bookkeeping, not wishful valuations that change at the drop of a hat. And our governmental institutions should reflect modern fiscal thought, not century-old Progressive canards. The credit-rating agencies' monopoly must be dissolved and a new free-market solution adopted to protect the investor. There was once a time, when Moody's Investor's Service, Standard & Poor's, and Fitch Ratings could be relied upon for their honest and truthful evaluations. The financial crisis proved that is no longer the case; in fact in 2015, the SEC fined S&P $58 million for fraud. Credit-rating agencies are supposed to be the backstop to protect investors, not a fox guarding the henhouse. A new credit-agency model must be constructed because the existing one remains broken and nonrepairable. If the government desires trust in the capital markets, then it must dismantle the existing credit-ratings agencies and adopt a free-market solution. Failure to do this will ensure another market collapse.

Clearly, there is no panacea that will cure the vulnerabilities still extant in our financial system. But implementing the solutions proposed in this chapter would at least be a good first step toward preventing another financial meltdown.

CHAPTER TEN

Observations

In past financial crises, major banks held most of the outstanding capital and could be brought together to develop a solution quickly. But those days are long gone. Today, US household debt exceeds $13 trillion, making development of quick solutions to crises very difficult. Yet transparency and disclosure remain critical elements in our free-market system. Accordingly, we must act now to end private exchange networks (the so-called dark pools) and other similar vehicles.

The troubling trend toward protectionism must also end. The protectionist era, culminating in the Great Depression, aptly demonstrated that when nations impose protectionist regulations, tariffs, and taxes to punish other nations (e.g., through the Smoot-Hawley Tariff Act), the "punished" nations will respond in kind. No one wins, but everybody loses. In contrast, if we seek to learn from and better understand history, we can use those lessons learned to develop safeguards and processes to protect our free-market system and to support innovation and entrepreneurship—while still holding nations accountable for unfair trade practices. Greed cannot be regulated out of existence, but it is possible to craft a legal framework that levels the field and holds its players accountable in the free-trade market.

Americans' savings are pitifully low, yet we continue to spend. No country that spends more than it earns can last long, yet easy mortgage equity withdrawals and other fast-money options daily tempt us to *spend*, not save. We must learn from history or we will continue to fall into these traps, both individually and in the aggregate—something we simply cannot afford to do.

If most of these CRA loans were written roughly a decade before the crisis, why didn't the market collapse earlier? Because when the loans were originally written, credit was still readily available, so consumers simply refinanced or took out home-equity loans to pay their adjusted loan payments, bills, and other expenses—that is, they robbed tomorrow's Peter to pay today's Paul. Flush with cash, many also succumbed to spending unnecessarily on things like new cars, home renovations, and luxury goods. This profligate spending spree kept the economy rolling along, but it masked the looming danger and delayed the inevitable: a credit-based "bubble economy," ready to burst. Everything was good as long as free money flowed and housing prices continued to rise.

Why *not* take out an interest-only loan, for example, if housing prices will never fall? "We can afford a *lot* more house, then!" Sure you can. Until you can't. Eventually the music stops, the bubble bursts, prices plummet, and interest-only debtors reside in homes they have no hope of affording. If you're paying only the interest on your mortgage, you're simply paying rent, in the form of interest. If your house value crashes, you still owe the entire note—the full price you agreed to pay for that house—in *addition* to the interest you continue to pay. This realization led many to panic and attempt to sell their homes in the sudden market slide, ultimately abandoning their financial obligations and declaring bankruptcy upon discovering there were no takers for bad investments. When the dust settled, the major financial institutions were left holding the bag—which meant the taxpayer was, too. The defaults rapidly expanded to a host of debt obligations, including credit cards, automobile loans, student loans, and commercial real estate debts.

With retirements increasing daily from the baby-boomer generation, the 2008 crash was likely simply a warning shot across America's bow. How do we expect to provide Social Security and Medicare benefits to seventy-eight million retiring workers from a country facing bankruptcy? These people earned their benefits, and we *must* honor our obligation to them. But where will that money *come from*?

CHAPTER ELEVEN

Hope Is Not a Strategy, Action *Is!*

With roughly ninety-four million Americans not in the labor force, the most important of the many important issues facing our country today is creating opportunities so all Americans can prosper. Real wages have not improved significantly in almost four decades, and the labor participation rate is the lowest it has been in thirty-eight years, while the cost of basic necessities like food, housing, medicines, and education have all doubled if not worse in the past three decades, placing tremendous strains on those least capable of withstanding those strains, such as those on fixed incomes, the young, the elderly, and the poor.

A vibrant economy can heal multiple wounds, but for many Americans the recession has not ended. Since 2016 many reforms have spurred economic growth, but we need to make those changes permanent and evenly positioned so all Americans will benefit. If wages do not significantly improve over the next few years, there may be an uprising of unimaginable consequences: political, economic, and structural.

During the Bush and Obama years, the federal government repeated many of same mistakes of the 1920s, '30s, and '70s, implementing the same failed policies—dressed up in more appealing clothing ("quantitative easing" and the like)—that continue to ruin millions of lives, particularly those of the retired and the elderly. The only true benefactors of the government's policy of printing money to pay debts were the banks and the federal government, so it should come as no surprise that millions of Americans are in still in economic misery or that they are losing out on countless new opportunities.

But what can be done? Hoping things will get better is no answer; we must take positive, real steps to turn this ship away from the raging storm and back into smooth waters. How? There are a number of ways we can steer America's economy back on track. We simply need to balance the needs of our nation's citizens with the needs of our nation's businesses. The following suggestions are offered as concrete strategies to save our country from economic collapse and to lighten the increasingly heavy tax burdens borne by the US taxpayer. Enacting these recommendations would go a long way toward delivering on the promises we owe the retiring generation as well as providing new opportunities and greater prosperity.

Repeal Obamacare

By definition, to *reform* means to improve or amend what is wrong or unsatisfactory. The only common ground in health-care reform is the perception that something must change. But what? Health-care costs are rising globally, it's true, but some countries receive a better return on their investment than others. In the US, for example, we spend two times more per capita on health care than any other high-income nation. The Health, United States, 2016 Report projected that by 2030, one in five Americans will be sixty-five years of age or older. That means these costs will only go up. Moreover, although the aging population is living longer, it has more chronic health problems. And though we might like health insurance to be free for everyone, such a Pollyanna ideal is cost-prohibitive. The tab is *trillions* of dollars per year, and *someone* must pay it. Based on the trend, that someone will be *your* children and *their* children. Is this really what we want?

Much of the focus on reform has been on how to make insurance affordable and accessible to all. The Orwellian-titled Affordable Care Act (ACA), a.k.a. Obamacare, was touted as the solution to the failure of health-care markets to provide coverage to those not sponsored under an employer plan, to those denied coverage because of preexisting conditions, or to those otherwise uninsured. Opposition to ACA stems from a host of objections. One is the fact that ACA was passed by Congress under cover of darkness. (According to then House speaker Pelosi: "We have to pass the bill so that you can find out what is in it." So we have to first *pass* the bill, *then* find out what is in it—do we have this right?) Another is the wealth-transfer mandate—that is, forcing anyone deemed to be wealthy and healthy to join the "risk pool" and to purchase health insurance to subsidize those with low incomes.

Health care for the acutely or chronically ill or injured is *very* expensive, and thus a coordinated effort to reduce the risk and cost of becoming ill or injured should be part of America's overall cost-reduction strategy. Of course, everyone favors cutting health-care costs . . . until *their* health care is at stake! Even so, were fewer Americans to develop chronic diseases, much more would be available to help those in need.

If there were a greater emphasis on primary care and preventive medicine, then expensive measures like chronic disease treatments, prescription drugs, and a host of other costs might be reduced or avoided. For example, lifestyle-intervention programs to prevent and reverse heart disease—such as the Ornish Reversal Program, as one of myriad examples—could be championed, encouraging the medical community and insurers to get on board with preventive (versus curative) programs, saving untold sums in treatments for preventable conditions.

Returning to Obamacare, out of the 14 million people enrolled, only 2.2 million are actually covered by the program. The remaining 11.8 million are actually covered under Medicaid. Politicians created over twenty thousand pages of regulations to take over the entire health-care industry and make it cater to 2 million people. It's also clear Obamacare was designed to fail. That way, statists—that is, those who believe government can solve every problem, as long as they control government—could then claim the only real way to bring costs down and raise quality of care is via a single-payer system. "Single-payer" is statist-speak for "Medicare for all," with the federal government—but ultimately, the taxpayer—picking up the tab. To control costs under such a system, the so-called Independent Payment Advisory Board was established under Obamacare. This board literally has the power of life and death over health-care recipients, for it has the power of granting or refusing medical treatment based on cost. If, in its infinite wisdom, this "death panel" decides the price is too high for the treatment requested, treatment is simply denied: "Sorry, Obamacare can't afford to keep you alive. You need to take one for the team." And, of course, those most in need of medical care—the elderly—will be completely unable to compete for services against younger, healthier recipients whom such panels will no doubt deem lower risks and better investments of the people's money.

America has the best-trained nurses and doctors in the world—not to mention the best-equipped, highest-tech hospitals—so how is it that our health-care system is ranked thirty-seventh in the world by the World Health Organization? Clearly, we have a problem delivering effective health care to the people of this nation. Costs continue to rise, yet we do not see improvement when it comes to keeping people healthy. This suggests our current model for delivering health care is unsustainable. We will never have enough money to pay for the ballooning populations of the chronically ill and aging. We need to radically rethink health care in America. Rather than focusing on treating or curing sickness, we need to build a prevention-based system focused on promoting wellness.

Can Obamacare help build such a system? No. Obamacare simply adds bureaucratic layers and expenses to the enormous health-care costs we *all* bear. Before Obamacare, 84 percent of Americans had health insurance. Even in a light most favorable to the statists proposing Obamacare, the solution to the health-care "crisis" would have been to provide insurance to the 16 percent having none, not for the Leviathan government to take over the entire health-care industry—a full sixth of the US economy! The real agenda: wealth transfer, from the haves to the have-nots. But in reality the have-nots get nothing—the corrupt statists take the pot. More than six million have lost coverage to enable two million to get coverage. Once the employer-mandate exemption expires, tens of millions more will lose their coverage—as well as their doctors. The "better" system will actually mean more expense, less access, and lower quality. Toby Cosgrove, former CEO of the Cleveland Clinic, noted that three quarters of all Obamacare enrollees face premium increases.

If the law actually helped our country, why did President Obama immediately grant Congress access to fifty-seven "gold" plans in the wake of Obamacare, yet force taxpayers not only to give up former benefits, but also to subsidize 72 percent coverage for Congress? Why should Congress be allowed to live under different rules from those it imposes over the rest of us? Why did Obama lie to Americans when he said we could keep our doctors and our existing plans if we liked them? Why did Obama grant over sixteen hundred exemptions from Obamacare to favored political allies, and why was he allowed to constantly change his law without congressional consent?

The answers to these questions are at once shocking yet unsurprising, in light of the rest of the revelations observed under the corrupt Obama regime. Obamacare was never about providing coverage to the 16 percent of the population who are have-nots; it was always about control and power over the health-care industry. Over twenty thousand pages of rules and regulations later, we are only beginning to understand the full extent of the metastasis of the cancer that is Obamacare. The simple answer to Obamacare is to get rid of it—before it gets rid of us.

Provide real health-care solutions
for *all* Americans

Obamacare must be repealed because it is suffocating business, health care, and the economy. Premiums and deductibles are pricing millions of Americans out of the market—they simply can't afford it! But the truth is, America does *not* have a health-care problem; we have an *insurance* problem. There is no competition in the health-insurance industry.

Why is it that regardless of the "reforms," the insurance industry always wins? Why is it that every industry sector seems to encourage the use of free-market solutions except for the health-insurance industry? It's time to break up the insurance monopoly and employ free-market solutions to the health-care-insurance problem. A good first step would be to publish prices for each procedure. How else would we know if our premiums are commensurate with the care we receive? If consumers can compare prices on almost all imaginable retail goods or services, why is it unreasonable to expect the same capabilities for health care? Another idea is to implement a fee-for-service system, using health insurance only for catastrophic illness (a similar scheme to those used in property- and auto-insurance sectors). Yet another is to allow physicians to compete directly in the free market against other health-care providers, as well as the drug and insurance industries.

Certificate of Need licensing laws need to be abolished. These laws hurt both patients and competition by creating quasi monopolies for existing health-care providers. These laws are in essence a government guarantee that existing providers and hospitals will not have any competition without them getting notice and the ability to challenge new entries into their market. These laws limit competition and quality, and raise costs in the health-care market.

Regardless of the actual reforms implemented, Obamacare is simply unsustainable.

One fact was known well before Obamacare came along, however: the government has a miserable track record with health care. Just look at all the problems with Medicare, Veterans Health Administration, and the Indian Health Service. Obamacare promised to make health care more accessible and affordable. It has delivered on neither. As to President Obama's claim, "If you like your existing [health care] plan, you can keep it," history has already rendered its verdict: it was a lie.

We need a fundamental change to the health-care status quo, one which focuses on better partnerships between the health-care system and individuals. We also need a system focused more on disease prevention because, in the long term, preventing disease is much less costly than treating it once discovered. The current "preventive" health care—mammograms, cholesterol screening, and the like—while valuable, is not prevention. Preventive measures—like programs for fitness, diet, and behavior modification (e.g., smoking cessation or nutrition awareness)—support long-term health and help Americans avoid behaviors leading to illness and/or disease.

We cannot maintain our current path. Health care will continue to be a primary fiscal issue for the foreseeable future. While on an individual level we can use our best efforts to optimize our health and wellness, collectively the nation must make judicious use of finite medical services. Policy makers must be steadfast in directing our complicated insurance marketplace. The future of our nation depends upon their decisions, which is why voter awareness of issues like these—as well as an awareness of the positions policy makers stake out on each of them—is critical. The hospital and insurance industry does not want transparency. And there's no one forcing them to provide it.

Cut through regulatory red tape, and reform social programs, taxes, and trade

Congress must regain its constitutionally mandated taxing, spending, and legislative authorities. Over the years, Congress has ceded more and more to the executive branch, causing budgetary chaos and damaging the fundamental separation-of-powers doctrine, the bedrock principle upon which the Constitution was drafted. This abdication of authority and responsibility has resulted in cross-finger-pointing in both the legislative and executive branches. The abdications have been intentionally fashioned to confuse from the start, thus shielding both branches from the full brunt of accountability rendered by the American public at the voting booth. But the American voter is not an idiot. Such obfuscations can only last so long; once the hoodwinked voter becomes wise to the ruse, he or she will not soon forget the fraud committed—accountability will show up in spades, as it did in the 2016 presidential election. Congress must return to passing an annual budget for approval or veto by the president, so that it assumes its rightful authority and responsibility, and so every agency will be on notice it must defend its annual budget or be ready to lose some or all of it.

All new legislation and regulations, from all government agencies and commissions, must undergo a tax incidence analysis to determine the societal impacts. There are too many unelected bureaucrats wielding the power of Congress by running administrative agencies (and subagencies) and independent regulatory commissions (or "agencies") within the federal government creating and implementing legislation, rules, and regulations. Over the years, Congress, the executive branch, and the Judiciary have ceded their constitutional powers to these agencies, and it has created a separate administrative state. As a result, Americans have been subjected to tens of thousands of new rules and regulations without congressional review. It is time for Congress to stop passing the buck and do its job. It must immediately regain its rule-making authority. If Congress does not approve of the new rule or regulation, then the rule does not go into effect. Second, Congress must amend the 1946 Administrative Procedures Act to allow presidents the ability to cut costly and unneeded regulations. Presently, rules and regulations cannot be revoked, only replaced by new ones. This logic only exists because we have elected representatives who have no desire to act in the public interest, only in their self-interest.

Federal regulation since 1950 has cost our economy millions of new jobs. If we eliminated harmful and redundant regulations, today's real GDP would be in excess of $30 trillion, not $18 trillion. Imagine how that would help the unemployed and contribute to reducing income inequality!

Instead, Congress creates winners and losers by adding new regulations and lengthening the tax code. Why does it do this? Because it's a quiet way for politicians to repay their contributors. Not only does this reprehensible conduct foster crony capitalism, it destroys the public's belief in the

capitalist model and fuels the drive of the millennial generation to socialism.

Regulatory and tax reform will be very difficult to pass
because it pits the citizens against politicians and their
financial backers, who want the status quo to remain in
place. If you ever want to see this on display, take a trip to
Washington, DC, and visit the halls of Congress. They are
filled with legions of crony capitalists and corporatists looking for taxpayer money. A quick glance at the surrounding
cityscape will provide you all you need to know about who is
benefiting from your hard-earned salary.

One way to accomplish tax reform would be to reduce
the corporate tax rate to a flat 10 percent, coupled with federal spending reductions with associated spending limits.
Simply put, while everyone has seen a reduction in jobs and
opportunity, the government has grown at their expense. It is
time to reverse this perverse equation and reduce the size of
the most costly, inefficient federal government in the world.
America does not have a revenue problem, we have a spending problem!

With the exponential rise in productivity through new
technology, hardware, and services, there is no reason why
the government cannot reduce its size and spending by at
least 10 percent every year. Doing so will help us maintain
our obligations to all our citizens, eliminate social Ponzi-
scheme programs, and regain fiscal sanity.

If any leader were truly interested in making our economy
fair for everyone, they would demand that the Congressional
Budget Office perform a tax incidence analysis for any new
regulation or tax.

Why does the government force jobs overseas when a
simple reform of the tax code would eliminate businesses'

need to move offshore? Allowing companies to use legal cash-rich stock split-offs (a merger-and-acquisition technique that allows a company to rearrange its assets to avoid paying taxes) and corporate inversions (relocating a corporation's legal domicile to a low-tax country, while maintaining most of its operations in the high-tax country of origin) hurts the very people the government says it wants to help. These legal provisions take away billions in tax revenue for cities, states, and the federal government.

Eliminate all tax expenditures (such as exclusions, deductions, deferrals, credits, and special tax rates); this would save the taxpayers over $1.6 trillion. Eliminating these loopholes levels the playing field for all companies, big and small.

Stop penalizing small companies through the Sarbanes-Oxley Act. Like many supposed well-intentioned actions, this government intrusion into the financial markets was crafted to prevent the fraud perpetrated by the likes of Enron, WorldCom, and Tyco International. The problem is that the thousands of new regulations have penalized small companies, making it difficult to transition from privately owned companies to publicly traded ones by increasing regulatory compliance and onerous rules that only large companies can afford. This act has not helped the small-business owners and their employees, but rather has impeded their ability to grow and to create more jobs and economic freedom.

Eliminate the personal income tax and replace it with a flat or fair tax. Not only will this help save millions of dollars and time spent by citizens on preparing their tax returns, it will also increase productivity, which increases the growth of our economy (GDP), thereby creating new jobs. The benefits of a flat or fair tax extend well beyond the obvious—simplicity and fairness—and help eliminate one of Congress's dirty little secrets. That secret is how Congress creates carve-outs or loopholes in the tax code to reward its wealthy donors and lobbyists. By creating a flat or fair tax, there will be few if any loopholes and less ability for Congress to use language in the tax code as a vehicle to reward their large donors at our expense.

Eliminate expensing of interest from loans and deduction of state and local taxes from federal income-tax returns.

Eliminate the tax benefit for a person accepting a government position that requires them to liquidate their investment portfolios because of conflict-of-interest rules. There has been a revolving door of individuals accepting government positions solely to avoid paying huge capital-gains taxes on their investments. Once in the job and with their savings of millions of dollars of taxes in their pockets, these individuals find reasons to leave their posts. You will often hear these individuals state that they do not embrace the policies of the administration or that they are leaving for family reasons. The real reason is they accepted the job not for public service but for self-service.

Welfare reform

Providing a helping hand to those in need is much different than providing a handout and creating dependency. Time-limited social programs coupled with work, educational, and performance requirements will move these citizens onto the road to self-sufficiency. One hazard of our social welfare programs is the impact on the marginal tax rate of low-income families as they transition to self-sufficiency by making more money from work. The increase in income is overset by the reduction in food stamps, health subsidies, and other programs. In essence, our social welfare programs create a disincentive to work. Whether this was the dark intent of the creators of these programs or not, it is undeniable. We need to help these citizens make the transition to self-sufficiency through improvements in the tax code.

It is always amusing to hear from those who support free trade, open markets, and capitalism until they have to compete. Then these same people, or groups, scream that their industry or business is essential to our national security and deserves protection.

If the world were truly supportive of open and free trade, then there would be no tariffs, no barriers, no subsidies, no waivers, no exemptions, no caveats! But the world is full of politicians, so we have to work within a paradigm that protects our national interests (our people), while increasing our competitive and comparative advantage.

Offshore repatriation

Allow corporations the ability to repatriate their offshore earnings without double taxation at a onetime 10 percent rate, provided the repatriated earnings are solely used for US job creation. Prohibit increases in executive salary or bonuses.

With the added revenue from implementing the above, our economy will grow and therefore provide us the ability to make investments in infrastructure, capital, equipment, and software.

Infrastructure improvements

Rebuilding the nation's infrastructure will help in the short term with unemployment, but it will not be the inspirational innovation that leads our country. We need to focus on creating a new paradigm for all elements of our society. One such effort will be to create a comprehensive energy strategy that truly changes how the world produces, distributes, and consumes energy. By doing so, we can solve important problems facing the country in three areas: jobs, energy independence, and foreign policy.

Energy reform

Energy acts as a leverage issue for both domestic and foreign policy. If we get that policy right, it will help solve several other very big challenges that face this country and the world.

By now, we are all painfully aware of the dangers of reliance on foreign oil. Driven by our need for oil, US energy policy has led to military ventures that have proven costly in both our blood and treasure. Take away the subsidies that the oil companies receive in terms of tax breaks, then factor in the cost of Middle East military action and government handouts, and the cost of gasoline would certainly be a lot higher. But maybe we need to experience that real cost to push us to real independence.

It is time to direct our American ingenuity and creativity toward policies that encourage and incentivize new energy sources and technologies. American energy companies have

made huge improvements in natural-gas exploration that
have brought the price of this clean-burning fuel to historical
lows. The US solar industry is on the rise, and entrepreneurial "smart" technology is revolutionizing energy conservation
in homes and businesses. We need policies that encourage
this kind of creative business thinking. No longer can we
continue to prop up a system that leads to costly wars and
environmental damage. We do not need to create more rules,
regulations, and policy, but to focus on the right policy that
enables free-market ingenuity to produce solutions, creating
new industries and new jobs in the process.

Eliminate the US Renewable Fuel Standard. Corn-based
ethanol is the most polluting, costly, and inefficient method
for making ethanol. It takes over four hundred thousand gallons of water to grow one acre of corn per year. Fertilizers
to grow this corn pollute our water supply. Corn-based ethanol is inefficient, because it takes 1.3 gallons of corn ethanol
to provide the same energy of one gallon of gasoline. Corn-
based ethanol takes 15 percent of our food supply to burn in
our cars. Corn ethanol drives up food prices because there
is less corn to feed the animals that rely on it. This results in
higher production costs, which result in higher food costs for
consumers. The obvious impact is on the poor, but it affects
all of us because it raises the costs of our social welfare programs that feed the poor. Corn-based ethanol only benefits
the farmers and the farm lobby, who have placed their own
interests above the country's. If we are supposed to be for free
trade and open markets, then we need to let the market dictate. If we want to continue with ethanol, then we should opt
for the most efficient, effective, and environmentally sound
method of producing it.

There is no energy panacea; a realistic energy plan is a combination of energy solutions, many of which are regionally specific.

We can do several things in the short term to lead us to energy independence, reduce emissions, and increase marketplace efficiency.

+ Smartly develop and produce energy with our own vast natural resources.
+ Convert all commercial vehicles to burn natural gas.
+ Reduce fuel formulations from 12 to 1.
+ Update and develop new nuclear-power facilities.
+ Improve CAFE (Corporate Average Fuel Economy) standards.
+ Export liquefied natural gas to our allies, especially in Eastern Europe.
+ Strengthen our energy partnerships with Canada and Mexico.
+ Rescind the EPA Endangerment Finding.

There is a lot of debate surrounding the Keystone Pipeline. This 1,179-mile pipeline will add to the existing 2.5 million miles of pipeline stretching across America. In fact, additional pipelines will be built in the future to reduce or eliminate the transport of fuel on railroads. The Keystone conflict is not about fossil fuels versus alternative energy; it is about where we as a country want to source our fuel. Do we want to rely on our own continent's resources or those of the Middle East? Why not support our number-one trading partner and neighbor, Canada?

This oil is coming to market one way or another, so why not be smart and follow the recommendations of the State

Department, the states involved, and the workers who need the jobs?

It is clear that we have the ability to reduce our long-term fossil-fuel needs. Currently, we consume between 8 and 9 million barrels of oil per day. Fossil and liquid fuels are primarily used for transportation. Until we change this, we are totally dependent on oil.

We need a strategy that plans for the future and takes care of our short- and medium-term needs. We cannot expect our country to rely on alternative energy when the solutions are either not yet available, insufficient, or completely nonexistent.

The absence of a plan is not an option!

Immigration: restoring order

Immigration is good for America, but it must be controlled through a legal process. Immigration is not just people coming to the US seeking a better life; it is a national security issue. There are people trying to enter America to harm our nation! Do not lose sight of this, because if we do, we do so at our own peril.

Absent a law-based system, we will have chaos that harms both American citizens and those wanting to come here seeking a better life. Without a strict legal process (as is found in almost every country in the world), those trying to reach America are often abused, mistreated, raped, and extorted. Some of those who do enter into America illegally find themselves in even worse conditions than what they left, such as sex trafficking, or being denied payment for their work and treated like modern-day slaves. America is growing and so is the world; this growth will require more workers. With low birth rates and a large portion of our population retiring, America needs more workers. This creates fertile ground for a thoughtful debate on comprehensive immigration reform, but before we can have this, we must first fix the immediate structural problems that exist with border security.

Our existing process has Americans furious because our politicians repeatedly boast about how they help enforce and protect the rule of law, and value all life, yet they knowingly and willingly are criminal in allowing and assisting illegal aliens and their immoral employers. Allowing "sanctuary cities" or the harboring of illegal aliens is nothing more than politicians thumbing their noses at law-abiding citizens. In essence, politicians are saying, "We can pick and choose the laws we want to enforce and those that we do not, but you must abide by all of them."

Both Democrats and Republicans are to blame for this national immigration mess because both want to benefit from these people at the expense of its citizens. Democrats want votes and Republicans want cheap labor. Democrats believe that based on history new immigrants vote Democratic, and therefore, the more they can do to bring them in illegally, the stronger a chance they have of winning elections. Republicans want to help reward their business supporters who want cheap labor to replace existing middle-class jobs. The replacement of a middle-class job with one held by an illegal immigrant would quickly translate into higher profits for the company and its executives. A recent example of Republican hypocrisy took place in June 2018. As Arnold Ahlert wrote in the *Patriot Post* on September 10, 2018, "E-Verify has existed since 1996. Last June, the latest effort to make it mandatory for every employer was rejected by the GOP-controlled House after members bowed to the 'concerns' of the agricultural lobby that claimed it would produce a worker shortage."

There would not be a worker shortage if employers paid a wage sufficient for American citizens. But of course, why do this when you can exploit illegal aliens?

Both parties' objectives have nothing to do with what is best for the country or for the immigrants, but rather what is best for them. This manipulation has created numerous problems and now has pundits on all sides blaming each other while each of us has to deal with the result.

Before we can restore order to our immigration system, we must first understand the history behind today's problem.

Helping those in need is one of the most important goals in life. But is our present policy of assisting and promoting illegal aliens really helping those in need, or is it a policy of manipulating people for political gain and suppressing wages for US citizens?

Brief history

Prior to World War II, migrant workers came from Mexico to work in California and the Southwest. When their work was finished, they returned home.

During WWII, the country needed every able-bodied citizen to assist with the war effort. As a part of this effort, President Roosevelt established a guest-worker program. This program provided the opportunity for Americans working in the agricultural industry to leave their jobs and assist in other roles to help the country during a time of war, while formalizing a guest-worker program between migrants in Mexico and Guam to replace those that left. The 1942 Mexican Farm Labor Agreement, or the Bracero (manual laborer) Program, essentially formalized a guest-worker program that had been going on for decades, if not longer.

Bracero helped match workers who were desperate for employment with employers who were eager to hire. But as with most immigrant work programs, immigrants worked under harsh conditions, for low wages, with no ability to improve working conditions, and they drove down wages for legal US citizens performing the same tasks.

The Mexican government was and still is a huge benefactor of legal and illegal immigrant laborers because the wages earned in the United States are sent back to their Mexican families, who in turn buy local goods and services. This is an enormous benefit to Mexico, and in fact today, the repatriation of funds back to Mexico is the single biggest contributor to Mexico's economy. If these funds were to diminish sharply, it would cripple the economy there. This is why Mexico and other Central and Latin American countries do not want an end to illegal immigration into the United States. Americans are essentially subsidizing these countries, and they know it!

How did a successful guest-worker program turn into a mass illegal-alien scheme?

In 1964, President Lyndon Baines Johnson (LBJ) cancelled the Bracero Program. Why did he do this? Politics.

LBJ was concerned that the diminishing populations in large, predominantly Democratic-controlled cities would affect his reelection. If these cities continued losing people, then the next congressional redistricting would eliminate existing Democrat-controlled seats—which in turn would lead to less support for LBJ. So in order to help Democrats and maintain his own power, LBJ created a way to manipulate migrants.

How did LBJ do this? The best way to get more voters was to make it easier for migrant workers to stay in the United States.

Until LBJ cancelled the Bracero Program in 1964, most migrant workers could not afford to live in the US, so they returned home after their work. But when LBJ became president, he created his "Great Society," mainly a multitude of social welfare programs that can be considered the largest federal takeover of states' rights in American history. These programs now have the federal government involved in almost every facet of our daily lives. As a part of LBJ's "War on Poverty" (an oxymoron because he placed more people in poverty by enslaving them to government programs, destroying the family unit and creating a disincentive to work), he created numerous programs to provide assistance to migrant workers. These programs were incentives for migrants to stay in America illegally because they now could afford to.

LBJ did not care about the effects of his programs on the people or the country; it was all crafted to give free benefits to people so they in turn would vote for him. His manipulation of immigrants placed in motion the mess we have today in our immigrant system. In fact, every one of his policies plagues America today: Medicare, Medicaid, and the War on Poverty; immigration, education, economic, and financial policies; and even local and state governments. LBJ created the framework for the federal government takeover of the Republic.

Every President since LBJ has used immigration policy either for votes or for cheap labor.

Acting on congressional immigration legislation, Presidents Ronald Reagan and George H. W. Bush legalized over three million illegal aliens. This was supposed to be a one-time act that would keep families together and be complemented by strict border controls. (Have you heard this rhyme recently?)

Unlike those Reagan and Bush executive orders, which were constitutional orders based on an amnesty law passed by Congress to provide time-limited immigration relief, President Obama acted unilaterally, without legal authority, and flooded the southern border with tens of thousands of migrants. This was not done to help the migrants or the country. It was a reincarnation of LBJ's policies, on steroids.

President Obama set the border crisis in motion with his speech in 2012 announcing that as long as illegal aliens met his conditions, they could remain in the US. He laid out this strategy in the Deferred Action for Childhood Arrivals (DACA) policy ("childhood" being misleading because under this unconstitutional executive order, the "children" could now be as old as thirty-seven in 2018).

This policy, along with discussions within Congress of granting amnesty to the twenty to forty million illegal aliens within our borders, accompanied by poor security, created the mess we have today at our southern border.

Further evidence that the administration planned and expected the border crisis was the revelation that the Department of Homeland Security solicited bids in January 2014 for a government contract for "Escort Services for Unaccompanied Alien Children" in expectation of the arrival of sixty-five thousand minors on our southern border without parents or guardians.

The Obama border crisis was an intentional act to overwhelm the US Border Patrol, so it would force the Congress into accepting his immigration policy. This not only disregards the rule of law; it places all our citizens at risk. This deceitful strategy was created in concert with others in Mexico, Honduras, Guatemala, and El Salvador, to foster a mass illegal-migrant crossing into America.

These migrants are not refugees; they are paying up to $10,000 per person to be smuggled into America from democracies certified as such by the Organization of American States. The governments of these countries, to which American taxpayers contribute hundreds of millions of dollars each year, foster illegal migration into the US because it is a great source of revenue for their countries and a source of their own leadership's personal wealth.

It's one thing to try to gain an upper hand in politics, but quite another when you cause the deaths of many innocent young people. The pawns in this game are the children traveling over two thousand miles in brutal heat with no food or water, led by rapists and drug smugglers, with the expectation that they can stay in America. It is then unethical to overwhelm our cities and towns, forced to bear the brunt of this disastrous policy that is nothing more than human trafficking of the world's most vulnerable: the young and the poor.

Americans are some of the most giving and forgiving people in the world. We can always be counted on for compassion and for helping our neighbors. Sadly, politicians know this and use it against us for political gain. This border crisis is just another example.

No one wants to see people suffering, especially children, but if we are already struggling because of a maelstrom of economic malfeasance (local, state, and federal), how can we accept more unskilled foreign labor on top of our already indigenous unskilled labor? How can our communities accept more people when they don't have the resources to take care of those already here? Why are we treating migrants from Central America differently than those from any other part of the world? Why are politicians and the media manufacturing problems when the middle class cannot make ends meet?

Steps for restoring order

1. The Fourteenth Amendment was specifically written to provide citizenship to former slaves following the American Civil War. It was never intended to be used, nor should it be, for individuals entering the country legally or illegally as a way to gain citizenship by having a baby while in the United States. The courts must immediately begin enforcing the Fourteenth Amendment and stop the granting of birthright citizenship ("anchor babies").

2. No federal funding programs will be renewed to cities, towns, municipalities, or states that are harboring illegal aliens. Elected officials of these cities will be prosecuted for violating federal law. No federal funds or programs will be accessible for illegal aliens.

3. Institute a total immigration ban until our borders are secure and we have an accurate account of all of the illegal aliens in the country. This will cause much consternation, but it is needed to help restore order. Presently, we

truly have no idea how many illegal aliens are in the US—twenty, thirty, forty million—no one knows. Although the figure of eleven million has been used for over ten years, its accuracy is highly suspect and here's why. As Arnold Ahlert wrote in the *Patriot Post* on September 10, 2018,

> According to the Immigration Reform Law Institute (IRLI), there were as many as thirty-nine million cases where names on W-2 tax forms did not match corresponding Social Security records—meaning millions of Americans have had their identities stolen, potentially by illegal aliens.
>
> This gargantuan level of mismatches occurred during the last four years of the Obama administration, and one is left to wonder whether the Social Security Administration was grossly inept—or quietly complicit.

In addition, a recent study conducted by three college professors—Yale's Edward Kaplan, colleague Jonathan Feinstein, and MIT's Mohammad Fazel-Zarandi—discovered that the number of illegal aliens in the US is between sixteen to twenty-nine million. But again, this is just an estimate. With the border being so porous, record-breaking border surges during the Obama administration, and the inability to track visa overstays, no one knows for sure. One fact we do know is the number is much greater than the eleven million parroted by those who are not interested in enforcing our Constitution and protecting American citizens.

4. All criminal aliens should be deported immediately, with their home countries bearing the cost of deportation and penalties associated with their crimes.

5. Once the Justice Department knows exactly how many illegal aliens are in the country, we will create an immigration plan that follows the rule of law, that recognizes the decades of political exploitation of its legal citizens and the illegal aliens, and lastly that reflects our compassion for every life. Once we have control of our borders and a complete understanding of how many illegal aliens are present, we can develop a solution. It is unrealistic to believe we can deport tens of millions of people, so one solution could be to provide residency but not citizenship. Citizenship should be a privilege, not a right! No one here illegally should ever be able to gain citizenship. There must be a penalty for the crime and a reward for those who have endured the legal process. We must stand fast to honesty and what does good, not to what is wrong and what feels good.

6. Congress must immediately implement the 1996 Illegal Immigration Reform and Immigrant Responsibility Act that established the parameters and appropriated funds for a foreign visa holder entry-exit system. In 2017 there were over seven hundred thousand visa overstays, many from countries that are not friendly to the US. Congress must protect our country and pass a law that makes a visa overstay a felony and prevent overstay violators from

re-entering the United States. The home countries of those who overstay their visas will be responsible for the actions of those citizens. Each visa overstay will result in the home country paying the US Treasury $25 million. This money will only be used to pay down our national debt. Also, each visa overstayer's home country will be charged separately for their deportation.

7. Once our new immigration plan is enacted, if any employers are found to be hiring illegal aliens, they will pay a penalty of $10 million per person and will be charged separately for those workers' deportation. They would be permanently banned from any participation in federal programs/contracts. Money received from these penalties will be used to pay down the national debt.

8. An illegal alien's home country will be responsible for their citizen's illegal entry into the United States. The alien's home country will pay the United States Treasury a penalty of $25 million per person. Money received from these penalties will only be used to pay down the national debt.

9. A new guest-worker program will be created to match temporary workers with temporary employers. The employer must ensure that the worker is self-sufficient and will not be a burden to society—which means the employer provides the worker with government-approved housing, health care, English-language training, and a salary and benefits equal to what a US citizen would receive. A guest worker will be authorized to work in the US for a total of five years. Once their work is complete,

they will return home. The number of temporary workers will be based on a formula tied to our U-6 unemployment rate.

10. The H-1B, B-1, and L-1 visa programs are laced with deceit. These programs must be reformed to address the needs of our highly skilled US citizens, while encouraging highly skilled foreigners to work in the US. For too long, corporations have used these programs to drive down wages of US citizens and exploit foreign workers.

11. Reduce the tax burden on US corporations in order to create new jobs in the United States. As the U-6 employment rate decreases, there could be an increase in H-1B, B-1, and L-1 visas.

We are supposed to be a nation of legal immigrants. We welcome everyone openly, but his or her entry into the US must be done legally; otherwise, we are no longer a country. Immigration is not just people coming to America seeking a better life, it is a national security issue.

America provides everyone an opportunity to realize their dreams, but those dreams cannot be given to you. You must work to achieve them. Every ethnicity in America at one time or another has been the minority. Every group has suffered, endured, and persevered. No group will tell you that it was easy, and in many cases their treatment was inhumane and ruthless. The key to success for every ethnicity was to cross the cultural divide, and once this was achieved, they reached incredible heights. But this can only be achieved through hard work and perseverance. America is home to the world's immigrants, but that immigration is based on the rule of law. We support and encourage every ethnicity. All we ask of you is to learn the English language, adopt our customs, and be moral and virtuous people. Through this assimilation will emerge a new sense of nationality and pride, and therefore what it means to be called an American.

A caveat. It is important to note that a major obstacle to any immigration reform exists because of the policies—or lack thereof—of numerous US presidents dating back over fifty years. Their policies of allowing illegal aliens to enter our country without retribution have caused illegal aliens to have the expectation that these past policies will continue. Illegal aliens expect to be granted the freedoms and liberties of legal citizens. This expectation could have standing in a court of law and upend any immigration reform effort by granting amnesty/citizenship to tens of millions of illegal aliens because our politicians have allowed it for so long.

Education reform
K–12

Several years ago, I spoke at a town hall meeting on education. One of the attendees was a retired gentleman who told the audience that he did not believe he should be paying school taxes because he did not have any kids in school. I replied that by using that logic, I should not pay taxes for the fire department because I do not have any fires at my house.

I can guarantee you that the day you are lying on a gurney in the hospital emergency room, you will be praying that the doctor looking over you is the most educated and experienced in the world. Paying taxes to help develop the next generation of leaders is an investment we all benefit from.

Education is the foundation of any successful economy and nation. It is deeply troubling that we have an educational system in which we spend several times more per student than most nations in the world but fail to rank in the top twenty in science and math. What are we doing wrong? Are we failing to learn from history?

We have placed our K–12 teachers in a difficult, if not failed, system with unrealistic goals. First, today's teachers are now put in an environment where they have to be a day-care worker, policeman, nurse, and more, in addition to being a teacher. In addition, teachers today no longer have the freedom to actually teach based on their students' capabilities and problem-solving skills, but instead are teaching kids to be test takers. This system of teaching tests is not helping students or our country. The problem with our K–12 educational system is not the teachers; it's the system, which has been overrun by the federal government. Programs like Common Core are not structured for students to achieve excellence; rather, they are teaching mediocrity.

Two things need to change. First, parents need to have greater participation in their child's education. Schools are not a dumping ground; they are centers of learning, and parents cannot abdicate their parental duties to teachers. It is the parents' responsibility, not the school's, that their children arrive at school prepared to learn and study. It is also the parents' responsibility to know that their family's personal information is being data mined by the government and software and social media firms. Politicians thirst for more control over citizens; they are accomplishing this by creating programs and legislation to mine a plethora of personal information that includes our children's attitudes, values, beliefs, and depositions. This data mining extends to children as young as preschool and allows third-party vendors access to this information via annual assessments delivered through Common Core and legislated through the Every Student Succeeds Act and the Family Education Rights and Privacy Act. Technology companies such as Google (G Suite for Education) and Facebook (Teaching Strategies Gold Assessment) are using partnerships with the government to exploit our children's and families' data. This exploitation is disguised under the auspices of "sharing of information for a better world" or "data-inoperability," none of which is true. Second, teachers need the freedom to teach their students problem solving, not test taking. Forcefully promoting a system that is politically based (Common Core), as opposed to educationally based, helps no one. Each state should be allowed to develop its own set of criteria and to let parents choose the system that bests fits their children.

College/university education

College student-loan debt is over $1.3 trillion, and it appears that the taxpayers will be forced to pay for it. The cost of education has skyrocketed in recent years (up over 1,100 percent since 1978). This is no coincidence, considering this increase began as the government got more involved in providing funding for higher education. As the government provided more and more assistance, colleges and universities raised their admission and tuition costs.

If we are honest, a better model is attainable. Students are free to pursue a degree in any area they want, but they have to realize that not every field of study is going to result in a job after graduation. False expectations hurt no one more than the family and the student who made tremendous sacrifices to attend college, only to find themselves in debt and the unemployment line.

Schools need to realize that if they are going to accept federal subsidies via student-loan programs, then they have a responsibility to produce a graduate who has a job waiting for them. Failure to do so results in a reimbursement to the taxpayer.

It would behoove educational institutions to join with businesses to produce graduates who meet the needs of today's society.

A truly innovative solution would be to have a marketplace where students and investors could join together, where an investor could provide a loan to the student for a reimbursement from future earnings.

Blunt reality

The real folly is that there is not enough money to pay off the US national debt. In fact, if you add up all the money in our money supply, you will see that even if the federal government confiscated every dollar in circulation, there would not be enough to pay off the federal debt.

Many think our financial system is the ideal standard for the world. The irony is, once we placed our financial fate into the hands of politicians and twelve banks and eliminated the gold standard, our system was doomed to fail. Only Argentina and the Democratic Republic of Congo have had more financial crises.

Americans must realize that the Fed has too much power over our financial system (virtually every recession in the postwar era has been caused by the Fed), and it is time to reform or dismantle it before it can inflict any more damage on our economy and lives.

Entrepreneurial Capitalism—an honest and achievable path forward!

I have spent almost my entire adulthood exposed to life in Africa, Asia, the Caribbean, Central America, Europe, the Middle East, South America, and the former Soviet Union. This experience provides me the knowledge to say that it is deeply troubling and alarming to hear many Americans, especially millennials, say that capitalism has failed and that the only path forward is to embrace socialism.

The call and support for some form of socialism comes almost daily from politicians and the media. Many categorize themselves as "progressives," a term misused specifically to make one believe that the group is working toward progress, when they actually are regressive trolls wanting to take away our freedoms and liberties. They describe ad nauseam how bad life is in America. It doesn't matter the day or the circumstance, these cultural dividers are constantly telling anyone who will listen that life in America is terrible because the rich have stolen from the poor and, as a result, control every aspect of our lives. So the only way to ever have a chance of success in life is through the benevolence of politicians.

This is a lie and a tool that politicians use to manipulate your emotions and then take advantage of you for their own political gain. The truth of the matter is this: there is no country on earth that provides you more opportunities, freedoms, and liberties than the United States of America.

A brief walk through history shows that communism and socialism have killed over a hundred million people. Present-day Venezuela is a perfect example of how a country that was once wealthy, educated, and free has become a living hell. Socialism has not provided, and never will provide, the freedoms and liberties that have been granted to all Americans by our Constitution. If it could, why are immigrants willing to risk their lives to come to America?

We have all been blessed with talents, and it's up to the individual to recognize them and choose to use them. Self-reliance is the key to success, not government control. As I stated earlier, I am not aware of any writings that say life was going to be or is easy. The reality is life is not fair, and if you believe that it should be, you will never reach your full potential because you will always feel like a victim. In fact, this feeling or belief of victimization is exactly what politicians and the media want to encourage because it emboldens their plan of centralized government control.

I do know that no matter one's circumstance, everyone, even the most destitute, has the ability to choose his or her path forward. Americans have no reason to complain, because I can assure you, we have been blessed to be born in a country that provides you more than most people in the world will ever have. It's time to look within ourselves and not to someone else to solve our problems.

Has capitalism failed us?

What I believe has failed us is not free-market capitalism, but rather a distorted, manipulated form of capitalism variously called crony or state capitalism.

Crony or state capitalism is when a politician, government, or an elitist determines in advance which companies or individuals will receive the winnings.

Since the late 1800s, the term *progressive* was used to hide a movement led by individuals (such as John Dewey and Frank Goodnow) who used the influence of educators and bureaucrats to manipulate people into thinking that the Constitution was an eighteenth-century relic and had no relevance in modern society. The Progressive movement was born in order to place power in elitist and political hands to create a dependent class. It has used the educational system, starting in kindergarten, to manipulate young minds into a warped philosophy that counters the beliefs and values that are central to the founding of America—namely, that Americans' rights are not "unalienable," granted by the Creator. Rather, they are rights that are given to you by the government or society in which you live and are determined by legislative authority. Therefore, the biggest obstacle to the Progressive agenda is the Constitution. This is why we have Progressive/liberal politicians trying to use government agencies to take away your constitutional rights.

We see the results of this today in our protection of private property, in our activities at schools, in the media, and in day-to-day interaction with colleagues. We have become overridden with a Progressive agenda that has damaged the soul of our country, where even free speech is under assault.

It seems that we have become such a reactive society that every facet of our lives is unsustainable. Do not be misled by terms like *diversity, inclusiveness, fair, common sense,* and *inequality.* Progressives use these terms to manipulate people into thinking that they are there to help you but actually are meant for you to conform—conform to the belief that centralized government dictates your path, not individual freedom and liberty.

The only thing holding you back is you!

The truest form of capitalism is based on entrepreneurship. The founders of our country demonstrated this and incorporated its tenets into the Constitution and other founding documents.

Entrepreneurial Capitalism is based on self-reliance, morality, and public virtue. It is using your God-given talent to create opportunity and prosperity for yourself and others. It allows everyone to achieve their dreams by using their unique skills and abilities. It helps motivate and energize the individual to seek out new and uncharted waters that are ripe for opportunity. As each individual achieves success using their own talents, that success becomes contagious, where others want to emulate it and achieve their own success. This begins the cycle of self-reliance and freedom.

This form of capitalism fosters what manipulating elitists and politicians fear most: an enlightened, educated, free, independent, successful citizen who has no need for self-serving, dividing peddlers, namely elitists and politicians.

Entrepreneurial Capitalism ignites the very flames that drove our founders to fight for independence—the drive for human freedom! It is this very freedom that we must steadfastly protect and defend, because we are constantly battling the political predators who are desperately trying to steal it from us.

Our founders were rightly concerned about placing too much power in a federal government. They knew that once a select group of elected representatives became drunk with power, extravagance, and celebrity, then tyranny would be just around the corner.

The world's problems are all solvable because humans created them. But the only way we can solve these problems is by unleashing ourselves from those who are doing their best to harm and manipulate us.

It's been said that a good defense is a better offense. Our offense is to prepare ourselves through Entrepreneurial Capitalism. If we all do this, our dreams will become reality and our problems a distant memory. ***It's your choice!***

ANATOMY OF A MELTDOWN

Connecting the dots that led to the global financial crisis:

- Quasi privatization of Fannie Mae and Freddie Mac
- Modified Community Reinvestment Act
- NINJA loans are created and issued
- Lender sells a loan to a borrower
- Lender sells the mortgage to an investor (private/GSE)
- Investor buys a CDS to protect their investment from an insurer
- 9/11 terrorist attacks
- Federal Reserve lowers interest rates to 1 percent to ignite economy and consumer spending
- Easy credit allows NINJA homeowners to refinance or take out home-equity loans; borrowers use this money to spend and to pay off new adjusted mortgage payment
- Economy slows and home prices decrease; some homeowners owe more than their home is worth; homeowners start to default
- Economy slows further due to high commodity prices, unemployment rises, and country enters into recession; defaults rise

- Subprime loans default in large numbers; exposed lenders/holders have massive losses, try to raise capital by selling off assets, go into bankruptcy or are taken over by another company or government
- Loan defaults: investor collects payment from insurer
- Insurer has too many payments; company collapses due to a lack of confidence and liquidity; government bails them out
- Global investors that hold any subprime debt lower earnings
- Exposed companies deleverage themselves by selling off good assets to raise capital; the massive global deleveraging causes an avalanche in the global stock markets
- More companies are affected; 1 million jobs are eliminated in the US in six months
- Unemployment rises, affecting the broader mortgage market of higher-quality loans; people who had strong earnings now have no job to make any payments
- The Federal Reserve and Treasury step in to bail out the financial community
- The bailout does not stop defaults or bring certainty to the markets

ABOUT THE AUTHOR

 Paul V. Rancatore is a twenty-nine year Air Force veteran last assigned at the Pentagon. He is a former congressional candidate, as well as an entrepreneur, business owner, and captain for a major commercial airline. His thorough research and unique experiences in the armed forces, business, and politics constitute the background from which he draws his assessment.

Contact the author at Paul@paulrancatore.com.

"Freedom is never more than one generation away from extinction. We didn't pass it to our children in the bloodstream. It must be fought for, protected, and handed on for them to do the same, or one day we will spend our sunset years telling our children and our children's children what is was like in the United States where men were free."
—Ronald Reagan